JAY'S TEN COMMANDMENTS

1. Be Patient

2. **Don't Rush**......You'll make mistakes.
3. **Don't Guess**.....You'll get into trouble.
4. **Don't Panic**......It won't help.
5. **Don't Click**.......Until the mouse pointer is in the correct position.
6. **Don't Continue.** When you're stuck; think about what you just did.
7. **Always Save** ...Every 5 minutes and know where you are saving to.
8. **Always Know**...The results of commands before executing them.
9. **Always Use** ....Computer terminology, it reinforces the learning curve.
10. **Always Locate.** The cursor before you make changes in your document.

FOR SUCCESS WITH THE COMPUTER™

JAY'S TEN COMMANDMENTS

1: Be Patient.

7. Always Save

10. Always Learn

E-mail and the Internet for Grannies

Using America Online®

Javad Saffarzadeh, M.S., M.A.

Information in this document is subject to change without
notice. No part of this manual may be reproduced or
transmitted in any form, by any means whatsoever,
without the written permission of
Javad Saffarzadeh.

JS Computer Center, Inc.
724 Elm Street
Winnetka, Illinois 60093
Phone: 847-501-2677
Fax: 847-501-5638
E-mail: jay@jslearning.com
http://www.TeacherTalking.com
© Javad Saffarzadeh
ISBN: 09700054-1-5
Library of Congress Catalog Card Number: 00-191989

Comments and questions are most welcome.

*The screen captures of AOL software are printed with the
permission of America Online, Inc. America Online,
AOL, and the AOL logo are registered trademarks
of America Online, Inc., in the United States
and other countries.*

Edited by
Jim Grubman

It is assumed that users of this book already have a basic understanding of the Microsoft® Windows operating system. If they do not, we recommend studying Introduction to PC and Windows, *the first book in the* Teacher Talking *series.*

This book is fondly dedicated to my students, all of whom have been the inspiration for this work. They have shared the unique gift of themselves with me; it is through this sharing process that my teaching grows.

Author Acknowledgements

Special thanks go to the following people: Susan De Longis, M.P.S., for initially editing the manuscript and for motivating me to finish the work; Jim Grubman, whose hard work at editing this new version of the text improved it further; Norwin Merens, for his, public relations, and proofreading support; Farhad Abar, PhD, for his helpful suggestions; my son, Arash Saffarzadeh, for his valuable input. Finally, I would like to thank my wife Shokoh for her patience; without her support, writing this book would have been impossible.

October 2000
Chicago, Illinois

About this Book

This book was written for those who need a clear and effective approach to the basics of computer learning. The language is intentionally aimed at the beginning student. Concepts and procedures are presented in a logical, yet simple, manner. Years of proven success in the classroom form the foundation of the techniques offered here. Many beginners face fear and frustration when entering the world of computers. The author makes the journey both comfortable and exciting.

TABLE OF CONTENTS

Section 1
Beginning Concepts

Notes:

The History of E-mail and the Internet

E-mail (i.e., electronic mail) and the Internet are forms of communication; in fact, these are two of the most common forms of human interaction today. The evolution of communication is as old as mankind itself. Mankind's ability to communicate started in the days when humans' only means of exchanging information with each other was to relay messages by walking to their message recipients. So, they first relied on their feet to carry goods or news from one place to another. It could take months to accomplish this.

People soon discovered they could use animals such as horses to transport messages to others more quickly. The time it took to send information decreased from months to weeks. Centuries later, with the invention of the train and the automobile, information could be sent over very long distances within days. Once the telephone was invented, days were cut to only seconds, and finally, with the introduction of computers and the Internet, communication was revolutionized to the point where information can now be exchanged globally in just milliseconds.

Computer Communication Before the Internet

Before the advent of the Internet, computers could communicate with each other b in the following two ways; these two methods are still used today.

1. Local Area Networks

Local Area Network (LAN) describes how several computers located in one building can be connected to each other through computer cables and networking software. One of these

Notes:

computers is called the **Server**. A server, which you will hear more about later, is the central or connecting computer that holds all of the information the other computers share. These other computers are called **Work Stations**. The terms **Master** and **Slave** are sometimes used for these two types of computers. However, I prefer to use the terms Server and Work Station.

2. Wide Area Networks

Wide Area Network (WAN) refers to two or more LANs that are connected to each other. These separate LANs can be located at great distances from each other, in different cities or states.

What is a Modem?

A modem is a device that connects a computer to other computers through a telephone line. The actual function of the modem is to convert digital computer signals (i.e., electronic pulses) to voice signals (i.e., analog or auditory sounds), and vice versa. By using a modem, you can connect your computer to a regular telephone line. When the computer signals convert to voice signals, we have **modulation**. When those voice signals are converted back to computer signals on the other end, we have **demodulation**. Put the first parts of these two words together, then we have the word **modem.**

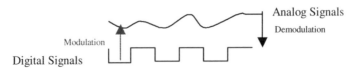

Analog Signals
Demodulation

Modulation

Digital Signals

Modulation/Demodulation Diagram

Notes:

The speed at which a modem operates is very important in facilitating fast communication between computers. Speed is determined by the number of small bits of information (i.e., bits or kilobits) sent or received per second. Speed categories for modems range from 28.8k to 33.6k or 56k—and there are even faster modems called Digital Subscriber Lines (DSLs), with speeds of more than one megabit per second. The faster the speed of a modem, the more efficient and easier it becomes to work online (i.e., on the Internet).

Online Service Providers

As modem technology entered the market, new companies known as **Online Service Providers (OSPs)** were established. Examples include **Compuserve®, Prodigy®, and America Online® (AOL).** These companies then hired large staffs to create huge databases, or electronic storehouses, of information in various categories, including news, shopping, weather, sports, etc. The OPSs also created communication programs that initially sold for $20–30. Once people began using them, the OSPs realized what a large source of revenue they could gain not only from the monthly fees that their customers (also known as subscribers) had to pay, but also from advertising items on their networks.

OSPs soon began offering their programs to subscribers free of charge to encourage more people to use them. If customers already had modems in their computers, they could easily install the programs into their computers themselves. The installation programs required users to open accounts to gain access to the providers' database programs. Since nothing is given away for free, subscribers had to pay $2.99–3.99 per hour to be online. Despite this charge, customers were very excited that they could sit comfortably in their own homes and

Notes:

check the news, buy airline tickets, check the prices of goods for sale, communicate with others through e-mail, and do much more.

What is the Internet?

 This is an illustration of the Internet, also known as "the Net." Each dot represents a computer, all of which are scattered all over the world, connected to each other. How are they connected? Exactly the same way that all telephones are connected, that is, through telephone lines. What is the Net used for? Its purpose is to allow people to share and exchange information, and to directly communicate with each other through their computers.

The Internet, which is really a "network of networks," was created in 1969 as the ARPA net, a project developed by the United States Department of Defense. Its initial purpose was to enable researchers and military personnel to communicate with each other in the event of a national emergency. Because of the complicated technology the Internet involved, it was initially unavailable for public use. In 1989, Tim Berners-Lee, an employee of the European Physics Lab in Switzerland, had an idea that revolutionized the Internet. He designed a program known as the **World Wide Web** (to be discussed more later). The purpose of his program was to make it easier for scientists around the world to share electronic documents.

Then, in 1993, the National Science Foundation's National Center for Supercomputing Application (NCSA) released a Windows program called **Mosaic®**. Later, **Netscape®** came to market. Netscape made it not only possible but easy for the average personal computer (PC) operator to use the Net.

Notes:

People worldwide were excited about using the Web. This created a big interest in its commercial potential for businesses of all kinds. Today, there is no way of knowing exactly how many people are using the Internet, because thousands more are joining the Internet community every day.

Providers of Internet Services

There are two types of Internet services providers: **OSPs**, and **ISPs (Internet Service Providers).** An OSP (e.g., AOL) has its own communication program that offers customers (or "subscribers") access to different types of information. Originally, OSPs existed only in the United States, but today, AOL serves many foreign countries, too. Once the Internet began to provide information internationally, the OSPs didn't like it, since this established competition with them. However, after they realized that people wanted to use the Internet, AOL and other OSPs added an internal connection into their programs that provided users access to the Internet, making these companies similar to ISPs.

Internet Service Providers

ISPs connect a user's computer to the Internet, just like a telephone operator. Therefore, ISPs don't need to have their own online programs—or the hundreds of employees required to run them. ISPs would provide the Internet program (e.g., Netscape) and local access numbers that connect their clients to the Internet. In the past, they charged by the hour for using the Net, and also charged a flat fee (usually around $20 per month), which still was cheaper than the rates charged by OSPs. In addition, ISP users could have access to the Net from anywhere in the world.

Notes:

This competition presented some serious problems for the OSPs. It meant that they had to bring their prices down, so they began charging users a flat monthly fee instead of an hourly rate. That is why in 1996 AOL announced a flat Internet usage fee of $19.95 per month. Because AOL had its own software (which was easier to use than that of the ISPs), this marketing move quickly motivated thousands of people into subscribing to AOL. Soon afterward, it reached a point where AOL could not handle the large volume of users, resulting in several problems: access numbers were constantly busy, paying AOL subscribers could not get online, and upset users couldn't even call the company in frustrated attempts to cancel their accounts. Eventually, after a lawsuit was filed against AOL and it lost the case, the company had to refund money to its customers. AOL was later able to resolve their problems by adding many more access numbers and more technical support.

Connecting to the Internet

There are two ways to connect to the Internet: **direct connection** and **dial-up connection.**

1. Direct Connection

A direct line allows you, as a customer, to lease the telephone line directly from a telephone company (e.g. AT&T, or Sprint), which means that you are always connected to the Net. So, your computer does not even need to dial an access number to get connected. This connection method works very quickly, but it is more expensive. The direct line method is used mainly by large entities like universities and governmental agencies. Recently, however, some cable companies have started to provide mass direct-

Notes:

line access to some residential communities with monthly rates as low as about $40.

2. Dial-up Connection

In contrast to the direct connection, a dial-up system requires you to first, have a modem, and second, sign up with a service provider—either an OSP or an ISP.

What are Access Numbers?

An access number is a telephone number provided to you by your service provider that computer modem dials to connect to the Internet. Normally, the access number is a local telephone number that you select from the list of numbers furnished to you by the service provider when you first register.

OSPs or ISPs—Which are Better?

The question of which type of provider is better depends on four factors: **connection cost, accessibility, technical support,** and **advertising.**

1. Connection Cost

This used to be one of the most important factors to consider when selecting an Internet provider. But since connection charges dropped to $20 or less, it is no longer a key factor. Some ISPs have even begun to offer free Internet access. One example of an ISP that markets this way is **Netzero.com**®.

Notes:

2.   Accessibility

Accessibility refers to the amount of time it takes for a computer to connect to the Internet. This depends on two factors. First, whether or not the telephone access number your computer dials is considered by your telephone company to be a local number; if it is not, you have to pay higher usage fees to the telephone company. The second consideration is whether it is easy to get through on the number (i.e., how often you get a busy signal when dialing).

3. Technical Support

Technical support (i.e., the online assistance often needed by Internet users) is a key factor for those working with computers. It is important to know that when you need help, you can get it quickly and easily. Sometimes, you may have to wait for long periods to talk to someone on the phone, and that person may or may not be helpful in solving your problems.

4. Advertising

Internet users face a constant stream of annoying on-screen advertisements whether they use OSPs or ISPs. This problem is often worse with providers that offer services to customers with no monthly fee.

Conclusion: When deciding whether to use an OSP or an ISP, consider all of the above factors and ask friends and business contacts about their experiences and preferences.

One advantage OSPs have over ISPs is that features such as chat room, buddy list, and e-mail all are combined within one program for easy use. Although the same features are

Notes:

available on most ISPs, they usually involve more steps to do the same things.

Therefore, most people consider OSPs easier to use. AOL (which is an OSP) is the most popular online provider in use today, especially for beginners and for families who use the parental control feature for their children.

Notes:

Section 2

Elements of the Internet

Notes:

Element of the Internet

Although there are many aspects to the Internet, we will concentrate on the four principal elements that you should know as a beginner. They are **e-mail; newsgroups; World Wide Web (WWW);** and **File Transfer Protocol (FTP).**

1. E-mail

E-mail works the same way as our postal service works, but electronically. When you send a letter to a friend in a different city, your mail does not go directly to that person. First, it is brought to your hometown post office, which then forwards it to your friend's hometown post office. Post office employees then check the address written on the envelope, and if it corresponds to one in their community, they deliver it to that home, business, or post office box. Your e-mail system works exactly the same way. If you are using AOL to send e-mail to a friend who uses CompuServe as a service provider, your mail first goes to the AOL computer or server. AOL's server checks the address, and forwards it to the CompuServe server, which looks at it and then forwards it to the recipient's mailbox.

In other words, when you go online to check if you have e-mail in your mailbox, you are connecting your computer to your service provider (in this case, AOL). If you have mail, it is actually stored in AOL's computer, not in your computer. This situation is similar to your being able to watch a network television program using any television set, regardless of your location (i.e., any location that is able to receive that network's broadcasting signal). This arrangement allows you to access your e-mail from any computer, anywhere, as long as it is connected to AOL. It also explains why your computer doesn't have to be turned on in order for you to receive e-mail.

Notes:

E-mail Addresses

To simplify and more easily identify e-mail addresses in the United States, all service providers and addresses are categorized by the nature of their activities. This system lets you know if you are sending mail to or receiving mail from a commercial entity, an organization, and so on.

Each category is abbreviated into three letters, placed after the period (usually called "dot" when saying the name aloud) that is near the end of the address. The most common abbreviations are as follows:

Category	Abbreviation	Example
Commercial	.com	aol.com
Educational:	.edu	uic.edu
Government:	.gov	nis.gov
Organization:	.org	church.org
Network:	.net	att.net
Military:	.mil	usa.mil

Therefore, if "golfball.com" is an e-mail address, it is clearly a **com**mercial entity's address.

Your e-mail address (i.e., **screen name**) is a name that serves as your electronic "address." You create it when you subscribe with a service provider. Normally, the screen name consists of up to 10 letters or numbers. The screen name can be anything you like, such as your real name, your street address, or any combination of letters and numbers that you like. Whatever screen name you decide to use, it must be different from the screen names of all other subscribers to your service provider.

Notes:

Domain Names

Another segment of your e-mail address is the **domain name.** The domain name is the name your service provider uses to identify itself. A good analogy is to think of an address on a postal service envelope. The address on an envelope can be divided into three parts: **Name, To,** and **Where.** For e-mail, instead of **Name,** you write your **screen name;** instead of **To,** you write the symbol @ (this is the uppercase 2 on your keyboard, which you get when you hold the Shift key and then press the 2 key); instead of **Where** you write the domain name (e.g., AOL.com). The following is an example of an e-mail address, Jsaff888@AOL.com., broken into the three key parts:

(Screen name) **Name**	**TO**	**Where** (Domain name)
Jsaff888	@	Aol.com

This shows that you are sending your e-mail to someone whose screen name is jsaff888, he is subscriber with AOL, and the e-mail address is that of a commercial entity.

Note: Never put a space between letters or numbers when keying in an e-mail address. For instance, in our earlier golfball.com *example, we did not hit the spacebar to break the words as you normally would: golf ball. An e-mail with spaces between letters, numbers, or words will be returned as "undeliverable" or say the "address does not exist."*

Tip: If you and your recipient both subscribe to AOL, there is no need to use the domain name— the screen name is enough, since you are both using the same server.

Notes:

2. Newsgroups

A **Newsgroup**, also called a user group, is an online group of people with a common interest in a certain subject (e.g., golf, music, etc.). There are thousands of such subjects, so there are also thousands of newsgroups to which you can subscribe, all with no additional charge. When you subscribe to a newsgroup, all of the communications and other information being exchanged within that group become accessible to you. When you send a message to the group, everyone in the group can read and respond to it. This process is referred to as **posting an article.**

3. World Wide Web

We have already talked about the history of the World Wide Web (also known as the Web, and referred to in written form and Web addresses with the letters **WWW**). But, what exactly is the Web? The World Wide Web is a program that makes available to you information of all types, such as text, pictures, sound, and even video images. There are two parts to the Web: **Web browsers** and **Web servers:**

Web Browsers
The **Web browser** is the computer software program that helps you find any information within your Web server (see below). There are different Web browsers available for you to use. One of the most popular ones is **Netscape Navigator**®, one of the first browsers that came to market in 1995 (the year the public began to use the Internet).

OSPs such as AOL, CompuServe, and Microsoft Network have been providing their members with their own Web browsers.

Notes:

Web Servers
This refers to all of the computer servers that hold all of the information that can be read on a Web browser.

4. File Transfer Protocol (FTP)

File Transfer Protocol (FTP) refers to the process transferring files from one computer to another. This function of Internet at the beginning was a very complicated. Today, however, all of the technical steps are already done for you. All you need to know is the difference between **Downloading** and **Uploading.** (We will discuss this distinction in more detail later.)

Section 3
Getting Online

Getting Online

Since most beginners use AOL, we have chosen this service provider's program to explain how to work with e-mail and use the Web (also called "surfing" or "searching"). Since the basics of using AOL are very similar to those of most other providers' programs, it is not difficult to apply these instructions to other online programs.

Installing the AOL Program

If you have an **AOL icon** on your computer or it appears on your program menu list, the program is already installed. If you do not have it, it can easily be installed. To do so, follow these steps:

1. Insert the **AOL CD** into your CD ROM drive and wait until a screen named **Install Screen** appears. This should take a few seconds.
2. Follow the **instructions on the screen.** If this does not work, continue with the following steps:
3. Double-click on the **My Computer icon** on your desktop.
4. Double-click on the **Control Panel folder** to open it.
5. Double-click on the **Add/Remove icon** to open it.
6. Double-click on the **Install button,** and then follow the instructions on the screen. *(See Figure 1 on page 38.)*

Note: It is important that you know the memory capacity of your computer (i.e., its RAM or working memory, and hard drive storage capacity). If you are using AOL version 5.0, you should have 32–64 MB RAM and more than 50 MB hard drive storage capacity. If your computer does not have this capacity, it might not be able to install the program. If you attempt to install the program without the proper amount of memory, it might work, but it is possible that your AOL program will work very slowly, and you could have many

Notes:

computer freeze-ups and other problems when you are online.

Figure 1

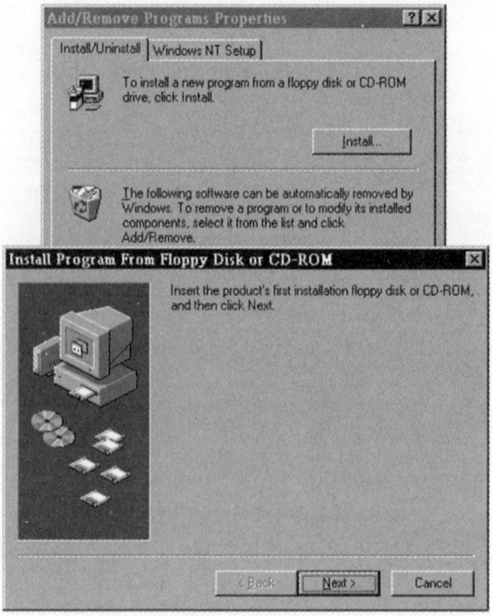

Notes:

Opening AOL

Note: First, make sure your computer is connected to the telephone's modular wall jack.

1. Double-click on the **AOL icon** on your desktop. If you don't have this icon, go through **Start, Program,** and **AOL** to open the program. You will see the **Sign On window** appear on your screen. *(See Figure 2.)*

Figure 2

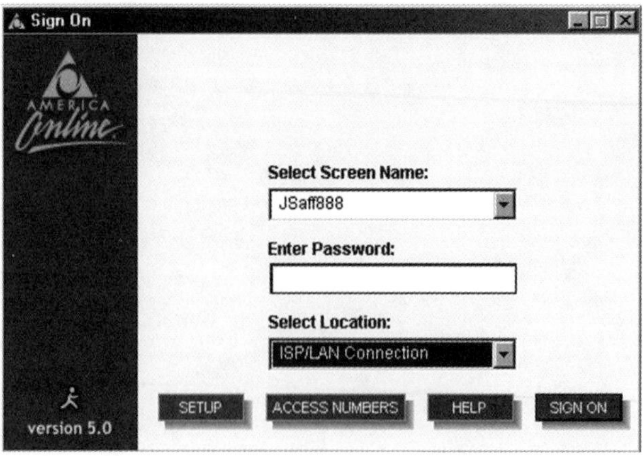

You should see your screen name in the **Select Screen Name field** or box. In AOL version 5.0, you can have up to seven screen names. In other words, if there are six other people listed in the same subscriber group, each can have his or her own e-mail "sub-address" to ensure privacy by creating a separate sign-on screen name for each of them. The person in the group who first registered with AOL and selected the first screen name used by the group has the **"master screen name,"** and therefore has the authority to add or delete other screen names for the group. If you have children, you can use AOL's **parental control feature** to

Notes:

block them from using certain features of the Internet. (This will be discussed later.)

2. If your screen name did not appear in the Select Screen Name field, Click on the **selection arrow** at the right edge of the box to see the list of all screen names, and then click once on **your screen name** to select it. *(See Figure 3.)*

3. Press the **Tab key** on your keyboard to move your cursor into the **Enter Password** field.

4. Type in **your password.** (Important note: Make sure no one is watching while you are typing in your password.)

5. Click on the **Sign On button.**

Figure 3

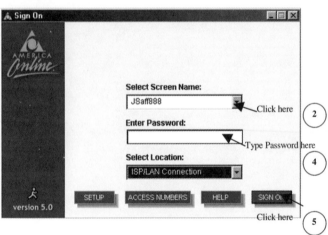

Notes:

You might hear some electronic connection noise and see some steps appear before you see the first screen or the main online menu. You might also see an advertisement screen asking you if you want to order some product.

Tip: You should not order anything at this stage. Just click on the **No Thanks button** *to return to the main menu screen.*

Move your arrow to any title. When the arrow becomes a **hand-shape**, this means that the item can be clicked on. Click once on an item to get more information under that subject.

Click on the **X** in the upper right corner of any individual window if you no longer need the window you are in, although it is not necessary to do this because you can move on to another window without doing so.

Notes:

Note: As mentioned earlier, AOL has its own online browser, which is different than the Internet browser. If you click on subjects that are not part of the AOL program, you will get to the Internet browser without even noticing. To distinguish between the AOL and Internet browsers, look at the top of the screen. If the Internet address (e.g., http://www.travel.com, or anything similar to that) appears in the address bar, you know that you are using the Internet browser.

Working Between Online Windows

After opening several windows, you might want to return to one of the previous windows. To do so, click on one of the small arrows at the top-left of the screen underneath of the menu bar. *(See Figure 4.)* To go to the previous window, click on the backward arrow key and to get to the next window click on the forward arrow key.

Figure 4

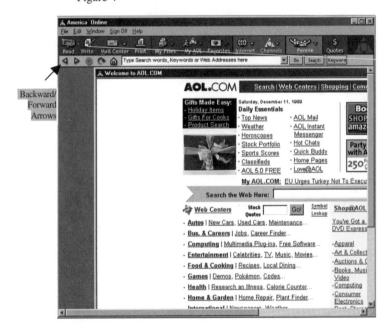

Notes:

Creating E-mail

To create e-mail, do the following:

1. Click on **Mail** or **Mail Center** in the menu bar.
2. Click on **Write Mail** or **Compose Mail** (depending on which AOL version you have). Now you are in the window where you can compose e-mail. *(See Figure 5.)*
3. Type the **recipient's e-mail address** in the **Send To box.** (If the cursor does not appear in this box, click inside the Send To box to get the cursor.)
4. Press the **Tab key** to move the cursor to the next section, which is labeled **CC** (or **Carbon copy** or **Copy To**). This section is used only if you want to send an additional copy of the same e-mail to someone else. If you do not wish to do this, press the Tab key again to get to the **Subject box.**

Figure 5

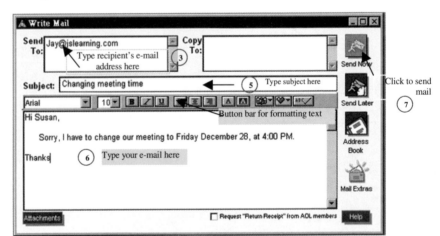

Notes:

5. Type in the **subject of the e-mail.** Your subject must be very recognizable or the recipient may delete it even before opening it. This is because people receive lots of junk mail every day.
6. Press the **Tab key** to move your cursor to the next section; this is where you enter the text (i.e., the "message" part of your e-mail). Type in **your text.**
7. Click on the **Send Now button.**
8. Click **OK** on the next screen. You've just sent e-mail!

Formatting E-mail Text

There are a number of ways you can change your text to make it look different (including making it **bold,** *italic,* or underlined). You can make the text align along the right or left edge, or the center, and even do a spell-check on it. You do this by following these steps:

1. Highlight **the desired text.** This is done by clicking to the left or right of the text, dragging the mouse pointer across the text you want to change, and letting go of the mouse. The selected text will have a black background.
2. Click on **the desired style-change option** in the button bar. *(See Figure 6 on page 52.)*
3. Click anywhere in the **highlighted text box** or press any arrow key on your keyboard to remove the highlighting and make the new style appear. *(To learn more details about formatting text, refer to* Teacher Talking Book II.*)*

ABC✓ **Checking E-mail Spelling**

Just click on the **spell-check button** and answer the questions in the **Check Spelling window.** The **Error**

Notes:

Message box will offer spelling suggestions. If a word you are spell-checking is not in the computer's dictionary, the computer will tell you that the word is misspelled. You can add that word into the computer's dictionary just by clicking on the **Learn button.** *(See Figures 6 and 7.)*

Figure 6

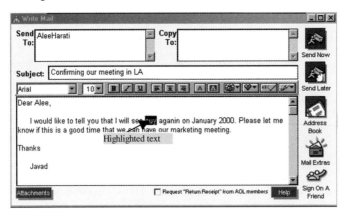

Figure 7

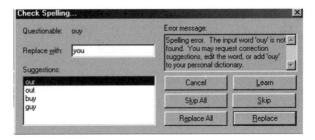

Notes:

Attaching Files to E-mails

Sometimes you might want to attach to your e-mail a
document that you have created in your word processing
program, or a picture that you have scanned into your
computer. It can be something that you have saved on your
hard drive or onto a floppy disk. To attach such a file,
follow these steps:

1. Create an **e-mail message** as directed above.
2. Click on the **Attachments button** located in your e-
   mail window. *(See Figure 8.)*
3. When the **Attach window** appears (this is the <u>second</u>
   attachment screen) click on the **Attach button.** *(See
   Figure 9 on page 56.)*
4. Locate the **file you wish to attach.** *(See Figure 10 on
   page 56.)* The procedure for finding a file is exactly the
   same as that for opening a file in your word processing
   program. (For more detail, refer to Book I of the
   TeacherTalking series.)
5. When you locate the file, **double-click on it.** You
   should see the name of the file appear at the top of the
   window in the fourth screen. *(See Figure 11 on page
   58.)*

Figure 8

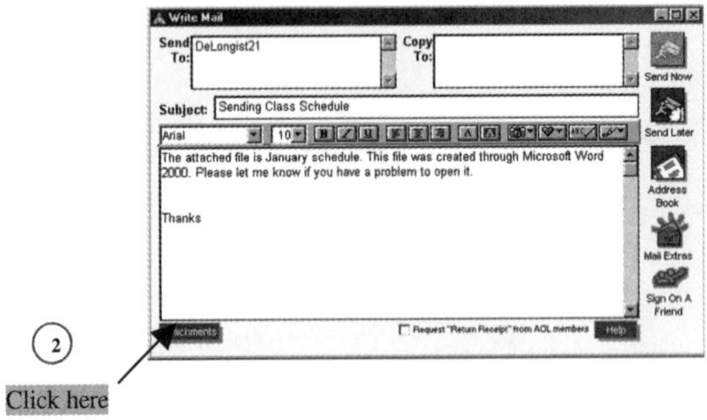

②

Click here

Notes:

6. Click on the **OK button**. You should see the name of the file appear **next to the Attachment button.** *(See Figure 12 on page 58.)* The on-screen location of the buttons can vary in different versions of AOL: some Internet browsers use a graphic illustration of a <u>paper clip</u> to designate Attachment *(see Figure 13 on page 58)*, but the steps will be the same as above.

Figure 9

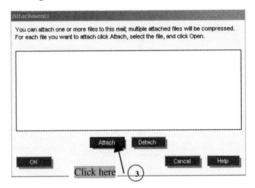

Figure 10

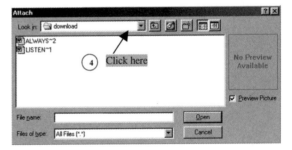

Notes:

Figure 11

⑥ Click here

Figure 12

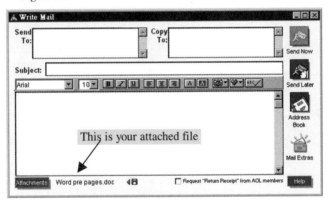

Figure 13

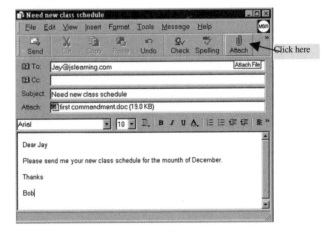

Notes:

Opening Received E-mails

If you have received mail, when you open AOL you will normally hear a voice saying, "You've got mail." (You will only hear this message if you have audio speakers connected and they are turned on.) Your mailbox icon also gives the same on-screen message by showing a small **envelope** in front of the mailbox icon. In addition, on AOL (or any other Web browser) you can Click on **Mail** or **Mail Center** in the menu bar and select **Read Mail** (sometimes called **New Mail** or **New Message** in other programs). You will then see the list of all of your e-mails. You can open an e-mail message by double-clicking on it. Or, you can click on it once and then click on the **Read button** at the bottom of the screen.

Note: When your are working on any online program, if your mouse pointer becomes a hand-shape it means that you can click once on the text or icon that the hand is on to open it; you don't need to double-click on it. Double-clicking while in the hand-shape mode might take you to the wrong screen.

Notes:

Printing E-mail

After opening an e-mail message, do the following to print
it:

1. Click on **File** in the Menu bar.
2. Select **Print** from the pull-down menu.
3. Click on the **OK button.**

 Alternative procedure: Just click on the printer icon
in the menu bar.

*Tip: To create multiple printouts of the same e-mail
message, highlight the desired number of copies in the
"Number of Copies" box, type in the number, and click on
OK.*

Notes:

Saving E-mails

The AOL system automatically saves received e-mails, but for only a limited time. To save your mail for longer periods, you can transfer it onto your hard drive by doing the following:

1. Double-click on the **e-mail you want to save.** You should see your mail open on the screen. (Do this step only if your mail is <u>not</u> open.)
2. Click on **File** in the Menu bar.
3. Select the **Save As option**; once you do this, the **Save As dialog box** will appear.
4. Type the file's name into the **File name box,** and select the desired location (i.e., the folder) into which you want to save the file. (For more detail, refer to *Teacher Talking Book I.*)
5. Click on the **Save button** in the Save As dialog box. *(See Figure 14.)*

Figure 14

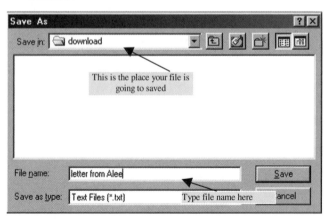

Notes:

Checking E-mail has been Opened

If the person to whom you sent your e-mail is an AOL
member, you can check your sent mail to see if the recipient
opened it. To check on your mail's status, do the following:

1. Click on the **Read icon.**
2. Click on the **Sent Mail button.**
3. Click on the **mail you want to check.**
4. Click on the **Status button.**
5. Click on **X** when you are finished.

Unsending E-mail messages

If your mail has not been opened yet, you can "unsend" it
(i.e., take it back). To unsend an e-mail message, follow all
of the above steps used to check your message's status,
except for step 4. After step 3, click on the **Unsend button**
instead of Status button. *(See Figure 15.)*

Figure 15

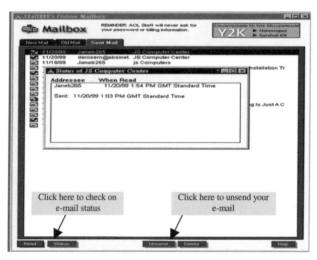

Notes:

Checking E-mail Using Someone Else's Computer

There are two ways you can check your e-mail by using any computer located anywhere in the world. These are **a) if the computer you are using has access to the AOL program,** and **b) If the computer you are using has access to any other browser than AOL.**

a) If the computer you are using has access to the AOL program, use the following steps:

1. Click on the **selection arrow** of the **Select Screen Name** box. *(See Figure 16.)*
2. Click on the **Guest option.**
3. Click on the **Sign On button.**

Figure 16

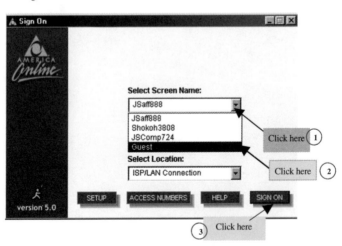

Notes:

4. **Wait** until you see the screen asking you to enter your screen name and password.
5. Type in your **Screen Name** and press the **Tab key** to move the cursor to the **Password box.** Then, type in your **Password.**
6. Press the **Enter key.**

You are now able to see all of your received or sent e-mails.

b) If the computer you are using has access to any other browser than AOL, use the following steps:

1. **Get online.** *(See Figure 17.)*
2. Type **http://www.aol.com** in the address bar.
3. Type in your **Screen Name** when you see a small sign-in screen appear.
4. Type in your **Password.**
5. Click on the **Sign In button.**

Figure 17

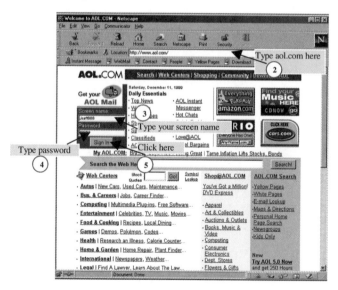

Notes:

You should now see all of your received or sent e-mails.

Note: Your Address Book will not be accessible when signing on from a different computer. This is because the contents of your address book are located on the hard drive of your computer and are not stored on the AOL server.

Notes:

Downloading Files

If someone has sent you an e-mail with an attached graphic file (e.g., a chart, table, or picture) or any other document type, you should be able to access and download it by using the **Download Now button** at the bottom of the screen. *(See Figure 18a.)* In some browsers, you might see the actual icon of the specific file. To download that file onto your hard drive, do the following:

1. Click on the **Download Now button.**
2. Click on the **Yes button** to confirm downloading.

Figure 18a

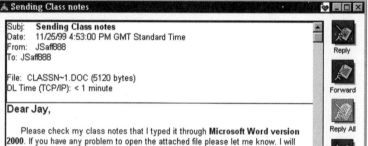

Notes:

3. The **Download Manager window** will appear. *(See Figure 18b.)*

4. Click on the **selection arrow** to the right of the **Save in box,** to select the folder name or location to which you want the document saved. (If you don't do this, the file normally will be saved inside the download folder under its original name.)

Note: Always be aware of where the file is saved to. Write the file's location down; if you forget where you have saved it, you will have difficulty finding it.

Figure 18b

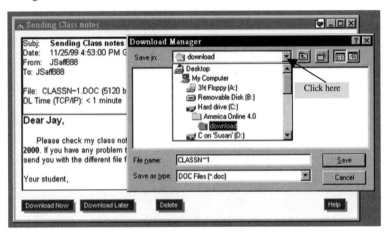

Notes:

Important Note: If you double-click on the downloaded file but cannot open it, it is because you don't have the necessary program you need to open the file. There may be some other ways to open the file. However, before discussing these, we must understand the concept of **file formats** (or **file types**).

File Formatting

As a beginner, you will typically be dealing with two file formats (or file types): **a) text files,** and **b) picture files.**

a) Text Files

When using a word processing program to type a document, you are creating a **text file.** The program used to create any type of file automatically adds its own formatting to that file. For example, if you are using Microsoft Word, your file content has a **Microsoft Word format.**

Note: Normally, if you create a file in Microsoft Word version 2000 and then e-mail this document to someone as an attachment, the recipient must have the same version of the same program in order to open the file without problems. If you don't both have the same version, certain procedures must be followed to successfully open the file. (We will discuss this in greater detail later.)

Tip: There is only one type of file format that can be read by any word processing program. It is called "Text, DOS, or ASCII File" format. Files saved under any of these formats cannot hold any styles such as bold, underline, margin, etc.)

Notes:

Making Files that can be Read with any Word Processing Program

(The following steps are based on the presumption that you have already saved the file while you were working in it. If not, you must first save it as you normally do. For more detail on how to save a file refer to *TeacherTalking Book I.*)

1. Open the **file** (if it is not already open).
2. Click on **File** in the menu bar and select the **Save As option.**
3. Click on the **selection arrow key** located at the right side of the **Save as type box.** *(See Figure 19.)*
4. Select the **Text Only option.**
5. Click on the **Save button.**

Figure 19

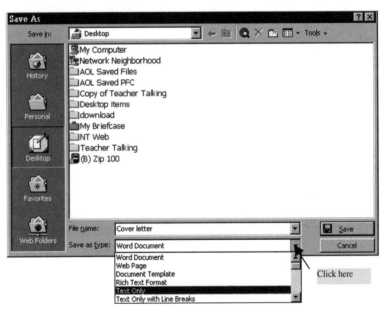

Notes:

Note: *You can save your file in other formats. For instance, if the person receiving your e-mail only has a WordPerfect program for word processing, select the WordPerfect format in Step 4 above. By doing this, your file is saved in the WordPerfect format—even if you are using Microsoft Word. This permits the person to open the file without a problem. The advantage of doing this is that the formatting you have applied—*<u>underlined</u>, **bold**, *or italicized text can remain in the file. A Text Only file cannot hold any of these formatting changes.*

Notes:

b) Picture Files

Picture or graphic files have their own formatting *(See Figure 20.)* You must have a graphic program that can read those files. Some of the well-known graphic formats are TIFF, GIF, BMP, and JPEG (or JPG). Some of these formatting types are more readable when using more graphics-oriented programs.

If your computer is loaded with the Windows 98 program, then you have the graphics program called "Imaging." If you have Windows 95, the graphics program is called "Paint." You can access either one if you click on **Start**, and select **Programs,** then **Accessories.** These programs let you open your picture files. New features in the AOL program now allow users to open picture files without going through these steps.

Figure 20

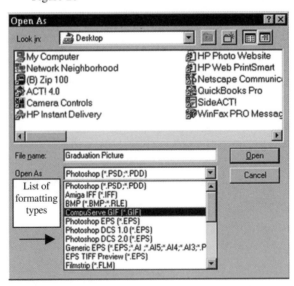

Notes:

Opening Mime or Zip Files

Sometimes, after downloading an attachment you received via e-mail, you might be unable to open it. Or, if you can open it, you might see some kind of "junk" text that doesn't make sense (i.e., lines of letters and characters that have no relation to each other, or might have no meaning at all). If you look at the file name, you will see the word **"Mime"** (or sometimes **"mme"**) or **"Zip"** as part of the file's name. These words indicate that the text in the file is compressed (i.e., more text is squeezed into a file to cut downloading and uploading time). You cannot open such a file by just double-clicking on it unless you already have installed a basic utility program called **"Winzip."** If this program is not installed in your computer, you must do the following:

1. Click on the **Keyword button.** *(See Figure 21 on page 88.)* A **Keyword window** will appear.
2. Type the word **"Mime"** in the box labeled **"Enter word(s)."**
3. Click on the **Go button.** (This connects you to the Internet web site.)
4. Click on the **highlighted words "Mime Help & Software."** *(See Figure 22 on page 88.)* (If you can't see it, scroll down until you do.)
5. Click on the **highlighted words "WinZip: V 7.0 SR-1 WinZip."** *(See Figure 23 on page 90.)*
6. Click on the **Download Now button**. *(See Figure 24 on page 90.)*
7. Click on **the Save button.** (This automatically saves the file into your download folder, unless you select another location at this time.) *(To learn more details about saving files, refer to* Teacher Talking Book I.*)*
8. Click on **OK** to complete the process.
9. Click on the **X** to close the WinZip and Mime windows.

Notes:

Once you have downloaded this program into your computer, no extra steps are needed to open Zip or Mime files. They will automatically be opened by your system.

Figure 21

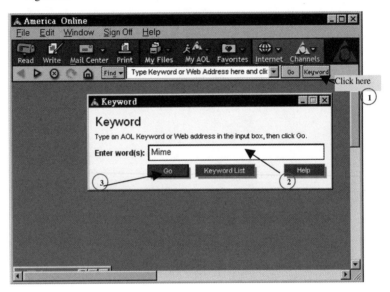

Figure 22

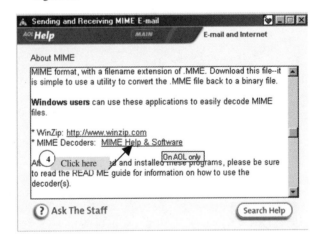

Notes:

Figure 23

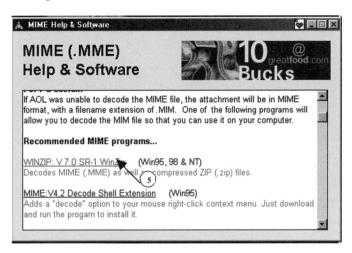

Figure 24

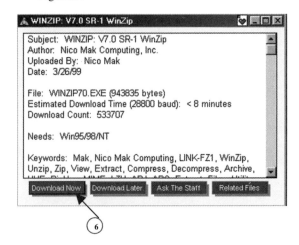

Notes:

Using the Address Book

The address book feature of your e-mail system enables you to store all of your frequently used e-mail addresses in one easy-to-use directory. One of the options available in the address book allows you to group e-mail addresses by separate categories. This is a very handy tool to use when you want to send one message to a group of people. If you want to invite all of your friends to a party, using the address book feature means that you don't need to create a separate e-mail for each of them.

Instead, you can create an address book group called "Friends," into which you can enter all of your friends' e-mail addresses. Then, after composing an e-mail message, simply select the Address Book group named "Friends." You will instantly see that all of the names in that group appear in the Send To box. Click on the Send button, and everyone in the group will receive the same e-mail. You can create groups as large or small as you like, under any category name desired. *(This procedure can be performed online or off line, which keeps your phone line free while you work.)*

Adding Individuals to the Address Book

To add a new person to your Address Book, do the following:

1. Click on **the Mail (or Mail Center) icon.**
2. Click on the **Address Book (or Edit Address Book) icon.** You will see address book window appear with several icons. *(See Figure 25 on page 94.)*
3. Click on the **New Person icon.** (In the older version of AOL you have to click on the **Create button.**) The **New Person window** will appear.

Notes:

Type in the person's **first and last names** in the applicable boxes. Then, press the **Tab key** to move the cursor to each successive box, and fill in the appropriate information. The only box that <u>must</u> be filled in is the **"E-Mail Address"** box; entering details in the other boxes is optional.

Note: If you and your e-mail recipient both use AOL, there is no need to type in the domain name; the screen name is sufficient.

Tip: If you see a section called "Notes," it is a good idea to take advantage of this feature by adding more information about the person. You might want to note the person's phone number and street address, or their business name.

Figure 25

Notes:

Adding Groups to the Address Book

The **New Group icon,** as mentioned earlier, lets you categorize all of your e-mail addresses into distinct groupings of your choice. To create a new group in your address book, do the following:

1. Click on **New Group icon** in the Address Book window. *(See Figure 25 on page 94.)*
2. Type the group's name (e.g., "Friends") into the **Group Name box.**
3. Press the **Tab key** to move the cursor to the address box.
4. Type in all of the individual group members' **e-mail addresses,** putting a comma between each address.
5. Click on the **OK button** when you are finished. *(See Figure 26.)*

Note: In the Group Name box, you must enter just the screen name, with no additional information. If you need more information than just a screen name, you should use the New Person icon to create a separate e-mail address for each person. You can also have one person in different groups. In an example like the above one, someone can be part of the group called "Family" and a group called "Friends" at the same time.

Figure 26

Notes:

Editing the Address Book

To change an individual's e-mail address, or to add a new
e-mail address to a group, do the following:

1. Open the **Address Book.**
2. Click on the **name of the person or group** that you are
   adding or changing.
3. Click on the **Edit icon.**
4. Make the necessary changes.
5. Click on the **OK button** when you are finished.

Deleting E-mail Addresses

To delete an individual's e-mail address, do the following:

1. Open the **Address Book.**
2. Click on the **name** of the person or group that you are
   deleting.
3. Click on the **Delete button.**
4. Click on the **Yes button** to confirm.

Using the Address Book When Writing E-mail

When you want to write an e-mail message there are two
ways that you can use your Address Book: **a) by opening
the Write Mail box screen first,** or **b) by opening the
Address Book screen first.**

a) If you open the Write Mail box screen first, do the
   following:

   1. Click on the **Address Book icon** located on the right
      side of the screen. The **Address Window** will appear.

Notes:

2. Double-click on the **name of the individual or group e-mail address** that you want to select. The selected address should then appear inside the **Send To box**. If this doesn't happen, double-click on the name again.

3   Click on the **X** located in the top right corner of the Address Book to close.

b) If you open the Address Book screen first, and then decide to write an e-mail message to any name listed in it, do the following:

1. Double-click on the **name of the individual or group e-mail address** that you want to select. This should open the **Write Mail window** with the screen name already typed in.

2. Then, type the **rest of your e-mail** as previously described.

Notes:

Junk Mail

One of the problems with online e-mail is that people become frustrated by the large amount of unsolicited junk e-mail (unwanted mail) they receive. According to AOL, they have already brought lawsuits against more than forty individuals and companies for sending junk e-mail to AOL and its members. AOL also is working with policy-makers at the State and Federal levels to develop public policies that address the practices of junk e-mailers.

A recent law passed in the State of Virginia was designed to go after the popular "spammer" tactic of using fraudulent and falsified return addresses. This legislation provides ISPs and individuals with stronger legal tools to use when pursuing junk e-mailers.

Stopping Junk E-mail

To eliminate, or at least limit, the amount of junk mail you receive, do the following:

1. **Report junk e-mail** by forwarding it to the screen name TOSSPAM. Reporting junk e-mail enables AOL to learn who sent it and to eliminate it. If your junk e-mail has an attachment from an unknown source, forward it to the screen name TOSSFILES.
2. **Use AOL's Mail Controls** to block e-mail from the Internet domains and e-mail address that you specify. To do this:

   a. Click on **MY AOL** in the icon bar.
   b. Click on **Parental Control.**
   c. Click on **Set Parental Controls.**
   d. Select the **screen name.**
   e. Click on **E-mail Control.**

Notes:

f. Select **Block E-mail** from the listed AOL members, Internet domains, and address.

g. Type the **unwanted E-mail address** on the right side of the screen.

h. Click on the **Add button.**

i. Click on the **Save button** when you are finished.

3. **Create a screen name just for chatting:** One way that junk e-mailers learn your screen name is from the chat room. When you use chat room, your screen name is on the list and everybody can see it. Therefore, you need to prevent your primary screen name from receiving junk mail that comes from this channel. To do this, create a **special screen name just for chatting.** Then use the **Mail Controls** to block all e-mail for that screen.

This is an effective way to block all junk mail to your primary screen name.

Important Note: Do not respond to junk e-mail in any way, even if you are asking to be removed from their mailing lists. If you do respond, it shows that you have read the message, and this helps to confirm your e-mail address to the sender. According to AOL, simply responding to a piece of junk e-mail can result in receiving even more junk e-mail. Another thing to remember: NEVER expose yourself to a potential computer virus by downloading any file that is an attachment to a junk e-mail!

Notes:

Section 4
AOL Features

Notes:

Favorite Places

When searching either AOL or the Internet, you will probably discover certain areas that you would like to return to when going online in the future. These are called "Favorite Places," and they can all be kept in the Favorite Places folder. By putting all of your Favorite Places into one location, you can access them quickly and easily.

 Adding Favorite Places to Favorite Places Folder

You can add the address of a Favorite Place to your Favorite Places folder by doing the following:

1. Go to the **site you like.** *(See Figure 27.)*
2. Click on the **heart icon** located on the top right corner of the screen that you are in.
3. Click on the Add to Favorites option. *(See Figure 28 on page 110.)* The online location you are in is now located in your Favorite Places folder.

Figure 27

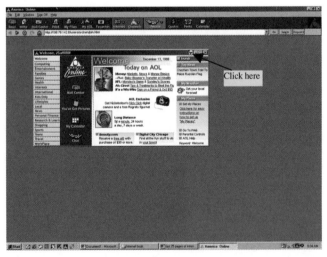

Notes:

Accessing Favorite Places

 Now, you can easily access these favorite places at any time, just by doing the following:

1. Click on the **Favorites icon.**
2. In the drop-down menu of places that appears, click on the **name of your Favorite Place.** This will automatically take you to the Favorite Place you have selected.

Figure 28

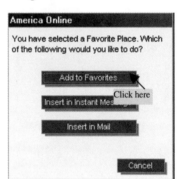

Notes:

Organizing the Favorite Places Folder

If you keep adding sites to your Favorite Places folder, it will crowd up the folder in the same way that your paper files would become cluttered if you piled all of them in one place. Accessing any favorite places will eventually become very time-consuming, because you have many stored in one single folder. To simplify the process of locating these favorite places, you can create folders within the main "Favorites" folder. First, you need to create a new folder. This can be done with the following steps:

Creating New Favorite Places Folders

1. Click on the **Favorites icon.** *(See Figure 29.)* The **Favorite Places window** will appear.
2. Click on the Favorite Places folder icon.
3. Click on the **New button.**
4. Select the **New Folder option.**
5. Type the **desired name** for your new folder.
6. Click on the **OK button.**

Figure 29

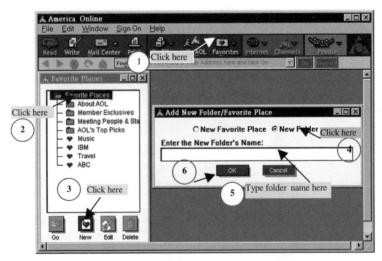

Notes:

Organizing Favorite Place Icons Within the Favorite Places Folder

To organize your Favorite Place icons within your Favorite Places Folder, do the following:

1. Click on the **Favorites icon** and select the Favorite Places option.
2. Click-and-hold on the preferred **Favorite Place** icon.
3. Drag the icon onto the **Favorite Places folder** you want the Favorite Place moved to. The folder becomes highlighted when you are on it.
4. **Release your finger** from the mouse.

Deleting Favorite Places

To delete Favorite Place icons from your Favorite Places Folder, do the following:

1. Click on the **Favorites Place** icon that you want to delete.
2. Click on the **Delete button**.

Notes:

Changing Names of Favorite Places

If you do not like an existing name of one of your favorite place icons, follow these steps to change the name:

1. Click on the **Favorites Place icon that you want to change** (in the Favorite Places window).
2. Click on the **Edit button.** A window with the Favorite Place's name appears. *(See Figure 30.)*
3. Type in **the new name** or **edit the existing one.**
4. Click on the **OK button.**

Figure30

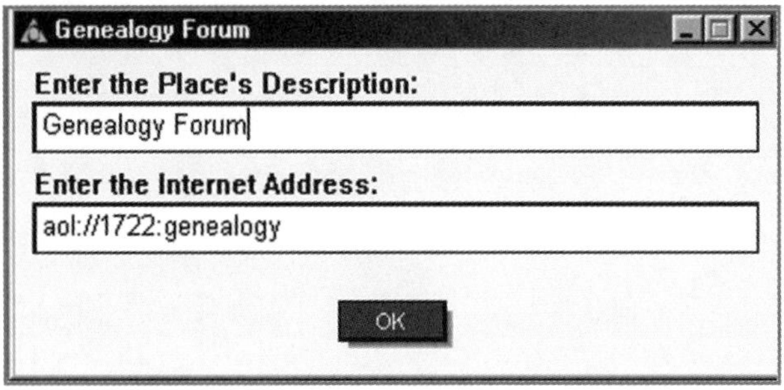

Note: In other Web browsers, the "Favorite Places" button has a different name. In Netscape, it is called "Bookmark." In Microsoft Explorer, it is called "Favorites," is located in the menu bar and it works exactly the same as in AOL's program.

Notes:

Changing Passwords

For your protection, no one but you should know your password, and you should not know the password of anyone else. If someone else knows your password and passes it along to another person, that person can use it to send mail under your name, potentially creating problems for you. Conversely, if you know someone else's password and a third person gets access to and wrongly uses the password, it is you who may be held responsible. Therefore, to maintain high security, it is a good idea to change the password every so often.

To change your password, follow these steps:

1. Click on **My AOL** in the tool bar.
2. Click on **Password.**
3. Click on the **Change Password button.**
4. Type in **your old password.** *(See Figure 31.)*
5. Press the **Tab key** on your keyboard to forward the cursor to the next field.
6. Type in the **new password.**
7. Press the Tab key again.
8. Since you just see asterisks (******) and not your actual password, for security purposes **you must type the password in again** for confirmation.
9. Click on the **Change Password button.**

    Figure 31

Notes:

Adding or Deleting Screen Names

In AOL versions 3 or 4 you can have up to five screen names. In AOL version 5.0 you can have up to seven.

To add or delete screen names, follow these steps:

1. Click on **My AOL** in the tool bar.
2. Click on **Screen Name.**
3. Click on the **desired option,** Create a Screen Name or Delete a Screen Name.
4. **Follow the screen instructions.** *(See Figure 32.)*

Figure 32

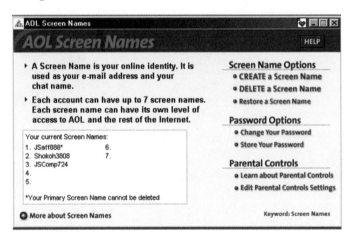

Buddy List

The Buddy List feature lists the screen names of friends and family who are online at the same time you are online, allowing for easy communication with each other. This can be done by using the Instant Message feature or by setting up a private chat room. You can add or remove people from your Buddy List group at any time.

Notes:

Setting Up Buddy Lists

1. Click on the **People icon** in the tool bar.
2. Click on the **View Buddy List** option. You will see a Buddy List window appear. *(See Figure 33.)*
3. Click on the **Setup button**.
4. Click on **Create**. *(See Figure 34.)*
5. **Type a name** that you want for your Buddy group, such as "School friends," "Old friends," etc.
6. Press **the Tab key** to forward the cursor inside the screen name, and type your friend's screen name.
7. Click on **Add Buddy**. You should see the name inside the Buddies in the group box.
8. Repeat Steps 5–7 until you are done.
9. Click on **Save**.
10. Click on **OK**.
11. Click on **X** to close the Buddy List windows.

Figure 33

Figure 34

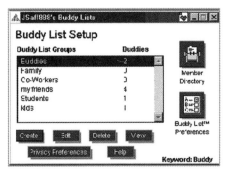

Notes:

Using the Chat Room Feature

Chat rooms are online, subject-based discussion groups. Being in a chat room allows you to communicate anytime with a group of people who are discussing the same subject. This is exactly like talking in person within a group of up to 25 people at the same time. There are countless chat rooms, all oriented toward different topics, and they are usually lively (although sometimes disjointed) discussions, since the participants are interested in the same thing.

To join a chat room, do the following:

1. Click on the **People icon** in the icon bar.
2. Select the **Chat Now option**. A screen will appear that has the name of a chat room currently in progress online. *(See Figure 35 on page 126.)*
3. Type words in at the bottom of the screen where your cursor is flashing. Just as you would do when you join a group of people in a physical room, you will usually begin with a greeting such as "Hi, everybody."
4. Click on the **Send button**. You will see the words that you have just typed appear on the screen among the other entries already there. (Your entry will have your screen name next to it.)

A person on the list might answer "Hi." You can then reply and continue writing and communicating with the other participants.

Notes:

Selecting Chat Rooms

To select a chat room topic you are interested in, do the following:

1. Click on the **Find a Chat option** located at the bottom right of the chat screen. The **Find a Chat window** appears, with a variety of subjects listed.
2. Double-click on a **desired subject**. This opens a window that lists various sub-topics, any of which you can select.
3. Double-click on the **sub-topic** that interests you, and you will be in the chat room you selected.

Figure 35

Notes:

Using the Instant Message Feature While in a Chat Room

 The Instant Message feature allows you to have an immediate and private conversation with another AOL member who is online at the same time you are. (Other chat room participants can't see this conversation.)

To have such a private conversation, do the following:

1. Double-click on the **screen name** of the person you want to talk to. (All the screen names are inside the small window located to the right of conversation window.) A small window with the selected person's screen name at the top will appear. *(See Figure 36.)*
2. Click on the **Send Message option**, and another box called **Send Instant Message** will appear.
3. **Type your message in the window.**
4. Click on the **Send button** to send the message to the person. *(See Figure 37 on page 130.)*

Figure 36

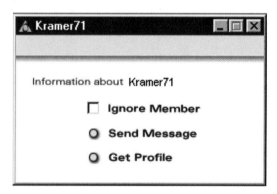

Notes:

Using the Instant Message Feature While not in a Chat Room

There might be times when you are online but not in a chat room, and you want to chat with another AOL subscriber. To do this, you can use the **Instant Message feature,** by doing the following:

1. Click on the **People icon** in the tool bar and select **Instant Message** from the menu.
2. Type the recipient's screen name in the **To field.**
3. Click on the **Available? button** to see if the person is currently online. If the person is not online, a message says that your party "is not currently signed on."
4. Type **your message.**
5. Click on the **Send button**. *(See Figure 37.)* Wait until the other person replies. You can continue your conversation as long as you like.
6. Click on the **Cancel button** when you are finished.

Figure 37

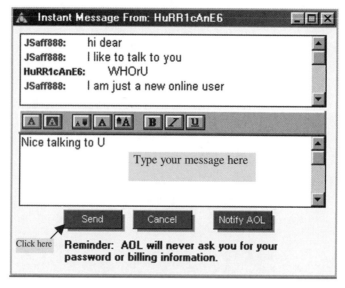

Notes:

Newsgroup

As we mentioned before, a Newsgroup is a group of people who have a common interest in one certain subject. To be part of any newsgroup, you must be a subscriber to that group; there is no charge for subscribing.

 Subscribing to a Newsgroup

1. Click on the **Internet icon** in the tool bar and select Newsgroup from the pull-down menu. This brings up the Newsgroup window with several icons.
2. Click on the **Add Newsgroups icon.** *(See Figure 38.)* A list of subject categories will appear.
3. Double-click on any **desired category**. You will see many options appear.

Figure 38

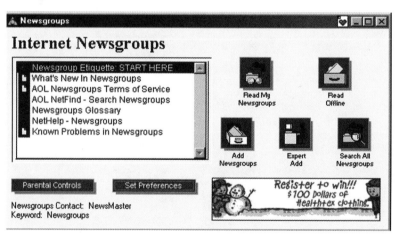

4. Double-click again on the **desired sub-category**. Continue selecting sub-categories until you see a **Subscribe button** at the bottom of the window.
5. Click once on the **desired subject** to highlight it.
6. Click on the **Subscribe button**.

Notes:

7.   Click on the **OK button.**

Using the Newsgroup Feature

You can **a) read your Newsgroup messages** and **b) reply to them.** To do this, do the following:

> **To read your Newsgroup messages:**
> 1.   Click on the **Read My Newsgroups icon.** *(See Figure 39.)*
> 2.   Double-click on the **desired category.** *(See Figure 40 on page 136.)*
> 3.   Double-click on the **desired subject to open it.** *(See Figure 41 on page 136.)*
>
> **b)   To reply to your Newsgroup messages:**
> 1.   Click on the **Reply button.**
> 2.   Type your reply in the **Reply window.**
> 3.   When you are done, click on the **Send button.**

Figure 39

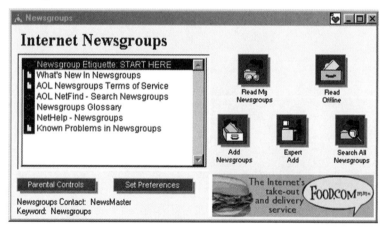

Notes:

Figure 40

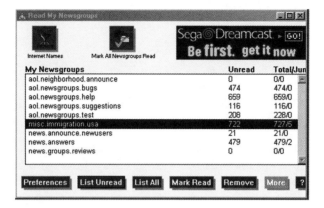

Figure 41

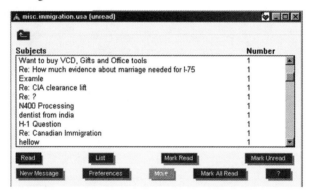

Figure 42

Notes:

Blocking Junk Messages from Newsgroups

To keep unwanted messages (i.e., advertising or other messages you don't want to see) out of any Newsgroup you subscribe to, you can filter them out by identifying the key words that usually appear in them. For instance, if you want to filter out messages relating to finances, you can use the Filtering feature to block all messages that have the word "money" in them. You can eliminate pornographic messages by Filtering out the word "sex" as well. To do this, do the following (when you are in the newsgroup screen):

1. Click on the **Set Preferences button.**
2. Click on the **Filtering tab.**
3. Type in **the words that you don't want to see in any of your messages.** *(See Figure 43.)*
4. Click on the **Add Filter button.**
5. Click on the **Save button.**

Figure 43

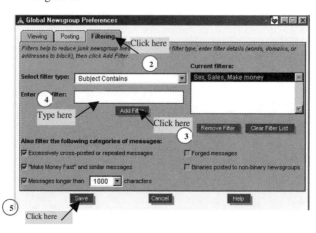

Notes:

Using AOL When Moving a Computer to a Different City

If you move your computer to another city and you still want to use AOL, you should change your telephone access number. If you sign on to AOL from your old location, you will quickly increase the amount you owe on your telephone bill. This is because any time you sign on to AOL in the new city and dial the access phone number located near your former home, it will be considered a long distance call.

To solve this problem, you should change the access number to one that is considered a local calling for the new location. This can be done by following the steps below. *(Note: This should be done when you are not online.)*

1. Click on **Setup.**
2. Click on **Add New AOL Access Telephone Number.**
3. Click on the **Next button.**
4. Type in the **area code of your new address.** A list of access numbers within that area code will be displayed.
5. Click on **Next.**
6. Double-click on **each telephone number** you wish to select, choosing a few that are close to your new location. (Choosing more than one number allows the computer to dial additional numbers if the first number is busy.)
7. Click on OK.

Notes:

Parental Controls

One of the best features of AOL is the Parental Control feature. (Compared with similar controls on other browsers, it is very easy to use, yet powerful.) The Parental Control can be set to only allow your children access to selected areas, including:

1. **E-mail**
2. **Newsgroups**
3. **Chat rooms**
4. **Web sites**
5. **FTP, and more**

There are certain parameters you can set in each area, such as the Filtering method just described.

Notes:

Using the Parental Control Feature

To use the Parental Control Feature, do the following for designated area:

1. Click on the **My AOL icon** in the tool bar and select Parental Controls.
2. Click on the **Set Parental Controls option**.
3. Using the select arrow key to the right of the Edit controls box, select the desired **screen name**. *(See Figure 44.)*
4. Under custom Control, click **on E-mail or any other options you wish**.
5. Select the settings you want in place. *(See Figure 45 on page 146.)*
6. Click on the **Save button** when you finished.

Figure 44

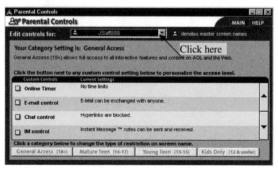

Notes:

Keeping Strangers from Sending E-mail to Your Children

To keep strangers from sending your children e-mail, do the following (when you are in **AOL Mail Controls**):

1. Choose **Allow e-mail from the listed AOL members, Internet domains and addresses.** The box to the right becomes active and the cursor becomes available to type in the e-mail address. *(See Figure 45.)*
2. You should **ask your child** to provide you all of his or her friends' e-mail addresses.
3. Type in the **e-mail addresses** of the people from whom your child <u>can</u> receive e-mails.
4. Click on the **Add button.** Repeat this process until all addresses are typed in.

From now on, your child cannot receive e-mail from strangers, but he or she can receive from all of the people whose names you typed in. This is something you should especially consider using for your younger children.

Figure 45

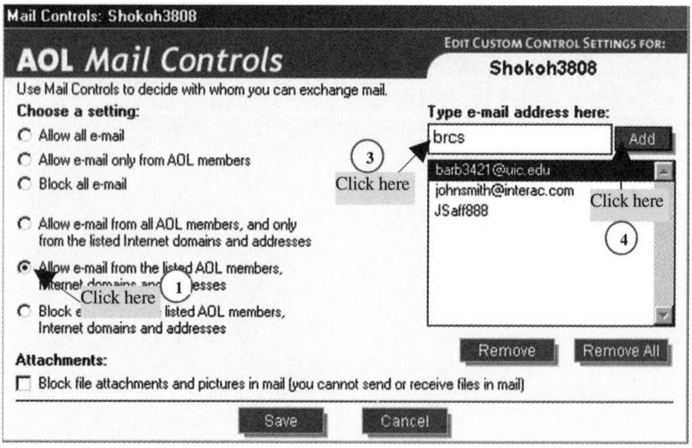

Notes:

To check if this is working, try sending an e-mail message to your child. If your e-mail address is not one of the listed names, you will see a message that indicates that the screen name to which you are sending e-mail is not accepting e-mail from your account.

Restricting Children from Using Chat Rooms, Newsgroups, and Some Web Sites

 To protect your children, you can limit their ability to access various online places. You can use the above procedure to limit access to Chat rooms, Newsgroups, and some Web sites, by following these steps:

Click on **My AOL.**

1. Click on **Parental Control.**
2. Select **screen name.** *(See Figure 44 on page 144.)*
3. Click on **Chat Control.**
4. Click on **desired option.**
5. Click on **Save.**

Notes:

Section 5
Using the Internet

Notes:

How to Locate Information on the Web

There are three ways to find information on the Web. You can do this by: **1) typing the address of the document** (to be discussed in more detail later), **2) using the search engine,** or **3) searching manually, category by category.**

1) Typing the address of the document or Web Site

There is a system you use to locate information in a library: each book has a reference number, and every page of each book has a page number. When you know how to look these up it is easy to find the information you need. We use a similar system to find Web documents. To understand this, you must first understand what Web sites and home pages are. We will use an analogy to help you.

What is a Web Site?
Let's assume that you want to create a brochure. You can design and layout the brochure yourself by using your computer, or you can hire a graphic designer to do this. After the brochure layout is finished, you can copy it onto a disk and take it to a printer. When the printing is done, you can distribute the brochures.

Now, using the Web, you can do the same thing, but instead of taking the disk that have your brochure on to the printer, you can take it to any ISP or OSP and ask them to place your brochure contents on their server. Once they have done this, you have a Web site. This process is also somewhat similar to having a television commercial produced: after production of your commercial is completed, you take it to a TV station so they can broadcast it to countless households. Similarly, once you have a Web site, it is instantly accessible to a very large audience, at less cost than making a TV commercial.

Notes:

What is a Home Page?
The first page of your Web site is called the **Home Page.**
Each Home page has a reference or an address to call or
retrieve. That is called the **Web address** or **URL.** The
following (i.e., the text in the Address box following the
letters URL) is an example of a Web address:

URL	http://www.nref.com/js

Address bar

This address, like all Web addresses, has several parts:

URL: (Universal **R**esource **L**ocator) If the URL shows up
on your browser, it normally appears outside the far left
side of the address bar at the top of the screen.
(See Figure 46.)

Figure 46

Notes:

Note: You may not see URL letters in some of today's Web browsers but see only the Web site's address. However, the entire address line is referred to as the URL address.

http:// (**H**yper **T**ext **T**ransfer **P**rotocol) This indicates that the server with the information you seek is a Web server.

www: (**W**orld **W**ide **W**eb) The name of most Web servers begin with these three letters.

To understand an Internet address, you should always read it from right to left; look at the Web address in the box below.

JS is the name of the file (e.g., a brochure file).
Since this is a commercial site, it uses **.com** in its name.
Nref.com is the server that holds the JS file.

Note: Never put any spaces into a Web address. Although you can use capital letters, it is always safer to use lower-case letter when typing a Web site. Connecting to a Web address is the same as dialing a phone number—as soon as you type in the address you are connected.

Note: Do not get confused between an e-mail address and a Web address. They have different elements, as shown here:

Jsaff888	@	Aol.com	E-mail Address
http	://	www.nref.com/js	Web Address

The @ sign is a symbol for an e-mail address.
The http://www is a symbol for a Web address.

Notes:

2) What is a search engines?

When using a telephone, you can get assistance if you do not have the phone number you need. You can call directory assistance, tell the operator the name of the person or business that you're seeking, and he or she can search for the phone number for you. There is some similarity here to using a search engine on the Internet.

A search engine is a program that helps you to find information that exists on the Internet. There are many search engines to help you find Web addresses and other information you need. Each search engine searches differently than the others (e.g., one searches only for new Web sites, and another searches through other search engines, etc.) But you must know the name, part of the name or some keywords of the document you are searching for. Some of the popular search engines are Excite, Alta-Vista, Lycos, Yahoo, etc. Later in this book, we will learn how to work with search engines.

3) Searching manually, category-by-category

Use this procedure when you don't know exactly what you are looking for, but you have some idea where to look and can take the time to search online. For instance, if you know you are looking for research data from a university that has an ongoing study of cigarette smokers, you can still locate the information.

First, click on the broadest category, (e.g., "education"), then click on the desired subcategory (e.g., "university"), then click on a narrower subcategory (e.g., "studies of cigarette smokers"), and so on, until you find the information you are seeking.

Notes:

File Transfer Protocol
File Transfer Protocol (FTP) means transferring files from one computer to another. This function of Internet at the beginning was a very complicated. However, today all of the technical steps are already handled. All you need to know is the difference between **Downloading and Uploading.**

Downloading Files
This refers copying a file from the Internet onto your hard drive. Let's say a friend has attached a picture to an e-mail that he or she has sent to you. When you download that picture to your computer, you are copying it permanently onto your hard drive or floppy drive.

Uploading Files
The opposite of downloading, this refers to sending a file from your computer over the Net or by e-mail to someone else's computer. Instead of receiving a file, you are sending one.

By using certain FTP features, you can sometimes download an entire program from the Internet.

Important Note: Downloading carries the risk of importing viruses to your computer. Unless you have an anti-virus program installed in your computer, it is not a good idea to download any free programs or files, especially if you don't know the sender.

Computer Viruses
A computer virus is a program that acts like a human virus (i.e., replicating itself and destroying normal system function), and there are many different kinds. Some computer viruses might have a minor effect on your computer, and others can have a major effect. Some might duplicate files, and others

Notes:

can delete your files and programs. They can appear in different places, such as in the memory or in the hard drive. Some anti-virus programs can diagnose viruses and remove them. However, some viruses are very difficult to remove.

A virus can be imported to your computer simply by inserting a floppy disk that already has a virus, or by downloading a virus-infected file through e-mail. This is why you should have an anti-virus program that can automatically detect a virus before you insert a floppy disk.

Notes:

Accessing the Web Through AOL

The Web browser is a built-in feature of the AOL software that allows you to access and view information located on the World Wide Web. To access the Web, follow these steps:

1. Click on the **Internet icon** in the icon bar. Select **Internet Connection** from the pull-down menu that appears.
2. If you know the Web address that you want to visit, move your **mouse pointer** to the end of the address bar http://www.aol.com. *(See Figure 47.)*
3. **Click once** to make the cursor appear.
4. Press the **Back Space key** to delete all the letters after **http://www.** (that is, all letters after the period).
5. Type in the Web address you want to visit.
6. Click on the **Go to the Web button.** If you don't have a specific site you want to visit, you can browse through a variety of subjects without typing anything specific. To do this, just click on the **Go To Web button.**

When you are on the Web and you move your mouse over any subject, you might see the mouse become a hand-shape. As mentioned before, this means that the subject or picture is accessible if you click on it once. This is called a link. When you click on a link, you get information about that subject.

Figure 47

Notes:

Using Search Engines

Just as there are several different types of "Yellow Pages" telephone directories, on the Internet there are also several search engines and directories. Although all of these directories do basically the same thing, each one searches for information a little differently and gives different search results, depending on which search engine being used. Some of the major search engines are Yahoo®, Lycos®, Excite^{SM}, and AltaVista®. Since Yahoo is the most-used search engine, we will discuss it a here.

Yahoo (which stands for Yet Another Hierarchical Officious Oracle) is the most famous directory on the Internet. Yahoo was started in 1994 by two Stanford University graduate students, Jerry Yang and David Filo. They created it to keep track of their many favorite Web sites. When other Internet users discovered their list and started using it, the directory concept became so popular that several businesses teamed up to sponsor Yahoo as a service to all Internet users.

To access the Yahoo Web site, perform the following steps:

1. Click once **inside the address bar.** This will highlight the words in the address bar.
2. Wait a second, then move the **mouse pointer** to the <u>end</u> of the highlighted text inside the address bar. When the shape of the mouse pointer changes from an arrow to an I-shape, **click once.**
3. Press **Backspace** to delete all the way up to the period after the www.
4. Type **Yahoo.com** here.
5. Press the **Enter button.**

Notes:

Once you have accessed the Yahoo website, you will see many titles that are underlined. As you move your mouse pointer over a title, the pointer changes to a hand-shape; this means that when you click on the highlighted word, information related to it will appear. If you have a specific subject you want to search for, just click inside the **Search Field box** to get the cursor. Then type in the words that describe what you are looking for, and press the **Enter key** or click on **Search button.** *(See Figures 48 and 49.)*

Figure 48

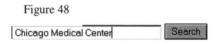

Follow the same procedure to use any other search engine. Each has its own Web address.

Figure 49

Notes:

How to Search for Information

Here are some tips to help you find information on the Web more quickly:

1. If you are seeking information about the Chicago Medical Center, but you don't know the <u>exact</u> name to type in, type **some of the words** inside the search field. *(See Figure 50.)* The search engine will look at every document that contains <u>any</u> of these words. Therefore, you will find a huge number of matches. Type it like this:

   Figure 50

   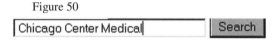

2. If you know all of the words in the title you're seeking but don't know their <u>correct order</u>, type in some of the words that you know (in any order), but put **one space, then a plus sign (+)** between each word (with <u>no</u> space after the plus sign). *(See Figure 51.)* The search engine will look for every document that has <u>all three</u> words in it. Using this type of search sometimes gets you documents that are not really relevant. If, for instance, you are searching for "Chicago Medical Center," you might get documents that talk about an "education <u>center</u>" in "<u>Chicago</u>", or a "music <u>center</u>" that is "owned by a <u>Chicago</u> business," etc.

   Figure 51

Notes:

To tell the search engine not to look for these unwanted words, put in the words for these categories after your desired words, using a space, then the minus sign (i.e., the hyphen) in the same way. *(See Figure 52.)*

Figure 52

Chicago +Medical +Center -music
Search

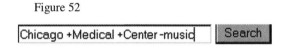

3. If you do know the exact title (and the proper ordering of the words), you can put the title or the phase inside **quotations marks.** The search engine will only look for documents that have the whole title (i.e., all three words in sequence) in them. This will give you fewer matches, but they will be more targeted for the results you want. *(See Figure 53.)*

Figure 53

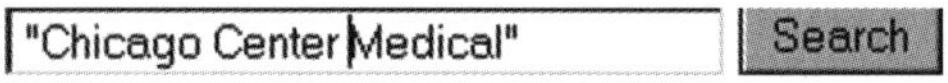

"Chicago Center Medical"
Search

When you get search results, the matches that are located at the top of the list are usually those closest to what you are looking for.

To learn how to search more effectively in each search engine, first get to the search result screen (usually the first or second screen provided), and click on the **Help link** located there. Then, just follow the tips provided.

Sometimes, if you scroll down to the bottom of the home page of the search engine, you will see a list of other search engines or links. At the end of the Yahoo home page, for example, there is a place that says “Yahoo Get Local.” First,

Notes:

click on it to get to that Web site. When you type a ZIP code inside the box that appears and press the Enter key, you will get all of the important information related to that ZIP code (e.g., maps, weather, education, business, and even directions on how to get there). This is a very good way to find maps and directions for many locations in the United States (and even some other countries).

Notes:

Printing Information from the Internet

When the information you are seeking appears on the screen, simply click on **File** in the menu bar, select **Print,** and press the **OK button.**

Saving Pictures from the Internet onto Your Hard Drive:

1. Position your mouse pointer **on the picture** and click on the **Right button.**
2. Click on the **Save Picture As option.** (You should see a Save As dialog box) with highlighted file name *(See Figure 54.)*
3. If you want to keep the original name for the picture, don't type it in. If you want another name, type the **new name.**
4. To find the file more easily, you might want to change the file location to your Desktop. Use the same procedure as that for downloading a file to do this; watch <u>and write down</u> where you save the file, so you can easily find it.
5. Click on the **Save button.**

Figure 54

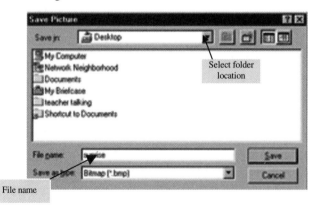

Notes:

Glossary

Bookmark   Valuable tools that enable you to quickly
                      redisplay useful information. Bookmarks are
                      not automatically erased when you exit
                      Netscape, as are the entries in the GO menu
                      and the History list.

Cache   An area in memory and an area on the hard
                      disk that are used by Netscape to store images
                      of the documents that you view on the World
                      Wide Web. If you return to a document or
                      graphic that is still in cache, it will load
                      quickly, since it does not have to be retrieved
                      from the Web server.

**Computer
Network**   Multiple computers connected in one of
                      several ways that enable users to
                      exchange information electronically.

**Content
Area**   The lower portion of the Netscape Navigator
                      program window that displays information
                      stored at the URL in the Location box.

**Data
Communications** The process of exchanging information
                      electronically over long distances using the
                      telephone or other data communication lines,
                      and special data communications software.
                      Also called telecommunications.

Dial-Up Connection

A type of connection service where a computer uses telecommunications software, a modem, and a telephone line to dial into an OSP or ISP in order to establish a connection with the Internet.

Direct Connection

A type of connection service where a computer uses telecommunications software to connect directly to the Internet through leased data lines.

Domain Name

The latter part of an electronic mail address or URL that contains the "address" of a particular computer and/or document stored on that computer (e.g., @aol.com).

Domain Type

A three-letter code that appears at the end of the domain name of Internet computers in the United States to help identify the type of organization that operates the server (e.g., com, edu, gov, int, net, mil, org, etc.).

Download

The process of receiving (copying) a program or file from a server.

Electronic Mail   A program to send and receive messages through a computer network.

FAQs   Frequently Asked Questions (FAQs) are files that contain the answers to the most frequently asked questions on a given topic.

FTP   File Transfer Protocol (FTP) is used to transfer programs and files between computers on the Internet.

Gopher   A menu-driven system of sharing information stored on the Internet.

Helper   Additional programs that can be installed on your computer to extend the multimedia capability of your Web browser program. Helper applications are usually simple programs that work with files that contain pictures, sounds, or motion video.

Home Page   The first page of a Web site. It can be the only page for the site, or it can be the cover page for hundreds of other pages of information within a Web site.

HTML   Hypertext Markup Language (HTML) is a word processing language that is used to create documents with HyperLinks, called Web pages that are stored on a Web server.

HTTP   Hypertext Transfer Protocol (HTTP) is used to locate and display information stored on a web server (e.g., http://domain name).

HyperLinks   A system of HTML pointers used to link documents together on the World Wide Web. HyperLinks enable users to display related information *quickly*, by clicking on a highlighted phrase or graphic.

Java   A new programming language used to animate Web documents. Java programs are called applets. They are small application programs that are automatically downloaded to your computer when you display a document prepared with Java, on a Web browser that supports Java. These applets run on your computer instead of the Web server.

Image Maps   An image made up of multiple hyperlinks that are programmed to display different information (e.g., a map of the world).

Internet   A *communications network* that enables people around the world to exchange information more rapidly and inexpensively that ever before, using TCP/IP and almost any type of computer.

ISP   An Internet Service Provider (ISP) provides access to the Internet, which contains many information services. E-mail services are also available. *(See OSP.)*

LAN   A Local Area Network (LAN) uses networking cables and software to connect two or more computers in the same physical vicinity. This enables people to transfer data from one computer to another and share expensive peripherals, like Laser printers.

Location Box   The box in the upper portion of the Netscape Navigator program window that is used to navigate to a specific Web page. To display a Web page, enter its URL in the Location box and press Enter (or Return).

Lycos   A Net Search program that enables you to find information on the World Wide Web.

Mailing List   A system of automatically distributing electronic mail messages to interested people called subscribers. A moderated Mailing List is screened by someone who decides which messages should be distributed to the subscribers.

Modem   Modem is short for **mo**dulator, **dem**odulator. A modem converts computer data into telephone signals that can be transmitted over the telephone lines. A *receiving* modem converts the telephone signals back into computer data.

Multimedia   The incorporation of pictures, motion video, and sound into documents and presentations. Multimedia on the Internet is also called Hypermedia.

Newsgroup   A group of people that read and post messages on a electronic bulletin board that is stored on a Internet News server and is dedicated to a specific topic of interest. *(See UseNet.)*

OSP   An Online Service Provider (OSP) provides electronic mail services, access to the Internet, and access to various *proprietary* information services, like sports scores, stock quotes, and the weather.

Plug-in   A more sophisticated program than a Helper application that can dynamically interact with Netscape. A plug-in program can be started automatically by Netscape, and the plug-in can also initiate actions within Netscape.

PPP   Point to Point Protocol (PPP) is one of two methods used to dial into the Internet with a modem. The other is SLIP.

Search Program   A program that enables you to search for information. There ar4e different Search engines for different types of information.

Server   Software on a computer that provides some type of information service (e.g., a Web server, FTP server, Gopher server, Telnet server, etc.).

SLIP   Serial Line Interface Protocol (SLIP) is one of two methods used to dial into the Internet with a modem. The other is PPP.

Status Line   The area in the lower left corner of the Netscape Navigator program window which displays various details while you are working.

TCP/IP   Transmission Control Protocol/Internet Protocol (TCP/IP) is the software communication protocol used by computers on the Internet.

Tele- Communications

The process of exchanging information electronically over long distances using the telephone or other telecommunication lines, and special telecommunications software. Also called data communications.

Tel\net

A program that enables your computer to access a Telnet Server through the Internet.

JURL

A Uniform Resource Locator (URL) is an address for a *specific piece of information* stored on the Internet. If you know the URL of a document you wish to see, you can use Web browser to locate and display it.

UseNet

A collection of News servers on the Internet that store electronic discussions on thousands of different topics called Newsgroups.

Web Browser

A program installed on a computer that makes it easy to access and display information stored on the World Wide Web by clicking on Hyper Links and entering URLs.

Web Crawler

A search engine that enables you to search for information stored on Web servers by entering keywords (when you don't know the URL).

Web Master

A professional person who is experienced with the Internet, with programming in HTML, and with designing Web pages.

Web Page

A document that is formatted in HTML and contains HyperLinks to other Web pages stored on Web servers on the Word Wide Web.

Web Server   A server that contains Web pages.

Web Site   A collection of Web pages on a Web server.

**World
Wide Web**   The World Wide Web is made up of all the
Web servers on the Internet

(WWW, or the Web)

A subset of the Internet. A Web server stores
multimedia documents that contain
HyperLinks. These links enable users to display
related information *quickly,* by clicking on a
highlighted phrase or graphic.

Index